My Empire Sputters

Will Reger

Cyberwit.net
HIG 45 Kaushambi Kunj, Kalindipuram
Allahabad - 211011 (U.P.) India
http://www.cyberwit.net
Tel: +(91) 9415091004
E-mail: info@cyberwit.net

Printed at VCORE LLP.

PREFACE

I always find it awkward to write about my writing, feeling that I am missing some important elements I should write about. When people ask what it is I write about, my shorthand answer is I am a nature writer. The natural world as a mysterious place where I can change and grow, where acorns crushed and consumed in a park can become a vicious remnant of the likes of Visby, and I can participate in some way as an angry cardinal, or frightened goose, or an old family mule. As a bear or a companion dog who bears its own worries about the world I travel through.

But there is so much more to what I write than nature. My work has been described as surreal by authors I respect, and accurate or not, I am happy to own that descriptor. It feels mysterious and hides my sense of smallness. What connects a tribe of faeries, which has found an Australian didgeridoo lost in the grass, to a mother calling her son in for the night and thus destroying an entire world, to a ditch with Titanic fantasies of a ship's orchestra going under in despair, to a man who wakes up disappointed he has not turned into a buzzard in his sleep because he forgot to sign the paperwork. The thing that holds these poems together is an element of suspended belief in which the poet has room to become or to act as he wishes, and the reader is invited to follow as he wishes.

Also, it is more entertaining to be surreal. That is where my mind will go: What is beautiful in nature? Can I be that beautiful? No. Something human will get in my way and wreck the fantasy. In a poem I can examine or change the parameters of reality and maybe see something new in the result

As a poet, I am a fan of language. I am also bound down by language, struggling always to find a way out of the patterns and habits not just of speech, but also of thought (and action) that language will impose. It isn't enough to describe a trip through Nebraska; I feel impelled to draw connections between the trip of the present and the journeys of the past, seeking some sort of deeper understanding of space or time or human relationship. In a poem, I can proctor an exam but then leave the civilized patrolling of the class to become a jackal-predator from some savage environment, liable to swoop down on the unsuspecting, taking a test. My threat to the "tender" students feels new to me. The language of being a proctor contains me, but I can wiggle out of the expectations. Now it is no longer, will I catch someone cheater; now it is will I tear someone's throat out? Maybe the smelly kid in the anorak? Only in the magic of the poem, of course. I do not deal in reality.

My poems extend the distant connections I have with people and creatures I know and, gradually lose through natural processes. My son who was not raised with any old cars to destroy in the backyard, my aging mother who served an ungrateful man with a buoyancy of spirit and a newness of technology, my cat who will get his belly rubbed. A man who suffers from cancer. A lady who is late for work because she has sicced her dog on a grazing flock of geese. I counsel astronauts not to make jokes at the expense of earthlings, yet I mock Superman for his get up. The discrepancy here is part of the surrealistic element of the exploration of character of these moments, part of the charm of the language that I use.

Contents

Nebraska is the Hours 7

Imago Mundi 8

Body 9

The Carnyx 10

A New Country 11

Battlefield 13

Faeries and Didge 14

To Be a Buzzard 15

How to Raise a Boy 16

The New Smoothing Iron 17

Common Courtesy for a Cat 19

The Sky is Falling 20

My Lady Arrived Late for Work 22

Ditch #4 Speaks to a Poet 23

Out Beyond CR '0' N. 25

How Like A Kingdom! 26

"Good enough…" 27

Don't Make Jokes 28

The Cardinal 30

Questo Momento 31

A Note to Clark Kent 32

The Nurse 33

So What 34

Ars Poetica 35

Black-capped Chickadee 36

Photo Shoot 37

Seaside 38

A Short Memoir 39

Tracking 41

The Gods of America 43

Dear American Gun Owner 45

Shooting Accident 46

Chimes 48

The Invisible Man 49

What Right Do I Have? 51

At Home 52

Evidence 53

The Egg 54

The Lonely Years 55

A New Day 56

Lily of the Field 57

The Fall of the Roman Empire: Another Account 58

The Wound 59

Bluebell Moon 60

Another Chapter in an Unwritten Book 62

Sequoia 64

The Loons' Death Song 65

Exam Proctor 66

Welcome 67

Shaw's Garden, 1974 68

Sixteen Modulations 70

Nebraska is the Hours

When I was young I crossed
the hillocky grasslands of northern Nebraska.
Everyone on that Greyhound
was hollow with the cold blindness
of being nowhere for awhile.

The sun stared in and none of us
understood how different we were
from the old ones of long ago,
who crossed these plains in conestogas.
We odd twenty-three random travelers.
We rode together having made one choice:
We bought a ticket and boarded.

We do not consider fire
or long hikes for wood or water,
nor do we fear the hanging shadows
or digging the tiny graves to leave behind.
The ones who track our line
through the grass or note our passing,
are like crazy dogs who chase us down
outside the smaller towns.

None of us trade our names to pass
on to loved ones back home
in the event we suffer a disaster,
If there was anyone who made it back.

Before us on our bus — nothing
but hours, heavy on our hands.

Imago Mundi

Here is a toy yellow truck
Tilted on a sand pile at the park.
The first drops of rain plink
On its scuffed metal cab.

It is what remains of a world
Of heroes, mountains, storm and bliss,
After a cavalry of clouds rode down
From the north to trouble the sky,

Then a mother calling
From a window—c'mon inside now!
And her boy runs home
Letting that world of his fall away.

Body

my empire sputters its days

age of time harbors years

my forest fire churns the world in jaws of flame,
a fire inside myself, the breath the world exhales.

my shot, my shell, my explosion
my smoke rolling in the sky, my high
darkness over the brightness of your field

engine to the future, my road into the distance
dusty with armies' march

tomb full of bones, my open gate, my wandering

my sky and trees, my exploration
my getaway car, my rain, my call to the breach
whatever it has to teach.

opening on everything

The Carnyx

It is a flower that rings
among the mountain stones.

A flower horn, god-like voice.
Graceful neck with elephant bellow.
The whine of zithers in mist.

Sea dragon, boar's head,
horse head, fish head open-
mouthed for prophecy.

Men of iron,
Celts in kilts
all scramble to battle,
screaming your song.

A New Country

I stand at the border of a new country.
I cannot see far into its heart of darkness
from where I wait, but the guard
is certain to wave me through in time.

I have no visa, no passport,
having lost that paperwork long ago.
I will enter this country and live here
without special permission, openly
like a local, walk its streets like I belong.

I will send you photos, of course,
letters, like this one, asking you
to come and visit and bring me things
from our old home, to remember and help
me navigate these new streets,
help with the confusing new laws,
help me confirm my gradual
citizenship in this country
with its continual confiscation
of my valuables and my energies—
even now I see that look you have
in your eye, that look of disbelief,
that says that you will never come here,
that it is madness to live in this god-
forsaken place.

How naive you look!
One day, my friend, you too will arrive

at this border and sit here in this anteroom
and wait to enter, and when the time comes,
you too will cross over humbly, a refugee
from your own life, and you will see
how so much changes once you get here,
once you are a citizen here, and you
will hear that old song echo in your ears,
"you can check out anytime you like,
but you can never leave!" You, too, will sit here
at the border and know it is the last border
you will ever cross and this country the last
to require your loyalty. We will die here,
and they will bury us as old men at the last.

Battlefield

Acorns broken over the ground
remind me of a hard battle.
The little caps tumbled around
as if knocked from warriors in battle.
The snapped twigs—their noble lances
driven into another knight
to shatter his tiny acorn hances,
the carapace or cuirass light.
It cracks and splits, falls to pieces,
exposing the white flesh to the world,
allowing the acorn to be squirrelled
away long after the battle ceases.
And where are all those heroes gone?
Not even the squirrels remember when
or where they interred the tasty bodies
of all those fearless acorn laddies
who feared nothing, but fell out the sky
to serve their oaken tree or die.

Faeries and Didge

When the faeries found a didgeridoo
Lying amid the leaves and grass—
How came it to fall into their holy place?—
They wandered into its heart, strange and hollow,

With a scent of eucalyptus in its throat.
Some told tales of once hearing its voice
While passing places known for human egress
And others spoke of the haunting words it wrote

In the night, the stories of gods and animals.
Yet none of the faeries thought it dangerous.
They gathered to inspect it, dressed as bluebells,
being both fashionable and curious,

Full of mischief, wondering if they could harness
the voice of the didgeridoo and make it speak
The things that faeries want to tell about,
The biggest faerie among them put his mouth
At the smaller hole and blew— he got a squeak,
And so, uninspired, they lost all interest.

To Be a Buzzard

If the earth could fashion me
Again with divine power
And a little mud, I would be
A Turkey Vulture next time,
My mate and I drifting over
Fields, deciduous woods,
Along iron tracks, wetlands,
Freeways and backyards.
Just for the view as we float.
The bird's eye view of life,
But sniffing for death below,
I'd know what the earth
Is eating in the spring,
Swallowing in summer,
Helped along by my kind
And the delicate beetles
Who pick in and out
The sweetness of decay.
Between us, the beetles and I,
We leave the bones glowing.
We are the shiny black things
Who keep the world clean.
We will wait in the dusk
For the earth to roll over,
Maybe forgetting to sign
The paper work for my transition,
so when I wake up I am still myself.

How to Raise a Boy

Raise your boy somewhere with old cars out back.
He will pay them no attention, except to note
they exist, and maybe one day he will haul them
off the property, calling them an eyesore,
a nest for foxes and mice, a den for addicts
or thieves, a danger to children playing.
Or he'll do nothing about it because he thinks of war
or business or love, or the environment or art,
or nothing at all, and rust and the weeds will hide
it away until another boy comes with a pain

he must get out by smashing old windows
with stones or bricks—he will dent the hood,
break out the lights, slash at the old whitewalls,
even set it afire or take shots with his .22.
Maybe it will be his hideout, his fort, or castle.
He'll make it his clubhouse or a private space
under the trees—even try to fix it, get it running.
A certain kind of boy even believes he'll drive it.
You can tell the man to come, by the way
a boy treats an old car on his property.

The New Smoothing Iron

It was not strange for my young eyes
to watch my mother do the ironing.
My father's shirts, sprinkled damp,
and one by one spread on the board
to be smoothed by strength of her arms.

Her electric iron was brand new,
but she could still wield the iron wedge
heated on the back of the stove
rumbling with the flames in its gut,
the way her ancestors did it.

One by one, with her electric
iron sliding and gently thumping,
she worked through the basket of shirts.
Every one was in white, smooth and bright,
so her man could turn out polished
in his dark three piece suit, red tie,
and shoes shined to a Semper-Fi edge.

A perfect encapsulation
of the war between the sexes.
She worked hard for him and perhaps
she understood his selfish airs.
I know she felt the buoyancy
spoken of by that Irish gent*
writing poems about his own
mother or wife doing such work.

I know she felt that buoyancy
because the entire time she sang.

*Seamus Heaney

Common Courtesy for a Cat

I hear a cat meowing among the trees.
He has wandered into a distance
he cannot, in my view, perceive.
Is it autumn with melancholy leaves?
Or winter with a killing snow?
No, it is early summer when the cat got out.
He won't be back in again because
he seeks something out there, and he is
guided by smell — or heritage —
who can say? I will always remember
the sight of that infamously gray cat,
hesitating in the upper branches,
and looking down upon the world,
beyond the reach of any sympathy.
Let him find his own way down,
if I must endure the same in life.
I will say farewell to him and take
my road deeper into the trees.
I have no words for this little one,
but if we meet again, I will rub his belly.

The Sky is Falling

Things fall from the sky:
Little balls of hard ice.
Arctic waves with searing cold.
Airplane engine parts —
even the airplanes themselves fall.
That Serbian stewardess fell
six miles and lives now with a limp.

Where are those stones from,
that enter our sky on fire?
One was caught on a dash cam
by a recent Russian driver.
And that Alabama woman hit
by a meteor while sitting
on her couch, remember?
It came right through the roof,
giving her a mighty bruise.

Take cover, they shout
in the movies. Stand in doorways
during the earthquake.
Get under the desk was the drill
when I was a kid in the 60's
during the nuclear arms race.

And how many bombs fell
on Hanoi, Dresden, London,
and every town in Japan?

All unleashed and hurtling
down upon our heads.

All these falling things are hard
to bear, but none of these fell
as hard on me as hearing the
news of your diagnosis. Not being
with you now, dear brother,
has been my meteorite-hail storm-
plane crash-bombing run-
nuclear disaster-fallout.

Precious boy, I can still smell
the scent of your hair.
I can still see your smile.
Part of you will always be mine
and part of me yours, no matter
what else falls into our lives.

My Lady Arrived Late for Work

She secured her hair with a scarf
And went to wait at the bus stop shelter.
I came along thinking it might be a game.
The sky might have been pearlescent or roseate:
Morning was coming on, like a grazing cow
Feeding along on the frosty grass of a meadow.
She stood under the shelter with her arms folded,
A pillar of disapprobation through the plexiglass.
An early fog had fallen in the park across the way
That mistook everything for an inferior version
Of what it might have been on a clear day.
The trees. The fountain, not yet turned on
For the season, the first tulips, already dismal,
And a flock of geese that had been foraging
In the grass, now settled with watchers on edge.
My lady kicked off her heels and crossed the street
Before I realized and I stood dumb before the sight
Until she called to me: "Astrix, come!" I passed her
Before even the watching geese felt unsettled,
But it was not long before they gave the alarm
And sleeping geese struggled to their feet,
Then took clumsy flight, higher and higher.
I leapt to catch one to keep as a pet for her,
But already they were too high and all crying
Out, regretting this disturbance of their rest.
My lady retrieved her shoes but missed her bus.

Ditch #4 Speaks to a Poet

If you want to speak for me,
poet, you must be water-minded.
You must write your poem
in algae and stone, in mud
sculpted by the glide of water.
You must speak in waving grass
how I descend the long prairie slopes.

But no, I think I'd better speak for myself—

My truest love is the prairie storm.
Great bosomy cloud banks
that dump their rain abundantly.

When all that water hits me
I feel something rhapsodic,
my runnels run in a dream
emerging in a ditch, pooling,
o'er-running the county roads
on my way to join the West Okaw.

Yes, I am only a drainage ditch.
I have no regard for myself.
All my words contain descent.
In falling, I speak. In speaking, I fall.

I am not even a slough or creek,
nor branch, nor river certainly.
I make no promises to anyone.

I do not irrigate anything.
My purpose is only to carry
excess water from the fields
and dump it into a small river
some miles to the south.

I perform that task well
enough that I am counted
fourth among ditches in these parts,
though in the hot months I do
nothing but meander between fields.

Sometimes in the heat, I sneak
among the weeds in my ditch,
sink into the ground, and rest
in the mud before I go on.

I am more mirage than miracle.
Even at my best I have never had
those glorious, oceanic,
silvery waves purling along.

I have never borne vessels,
no yacht or liner, not even
a toy boat. And that is just.
I am a creature of labor, not play.

Still, I fantasize that I am known as "The Ditch,"
the way the Atlantic is called "The Pond,"
and I would love to swallow the Titanic,
just to hear the desperation
in the orchestra's final hymn.
But I am only a ditch. Ditch #4

Out Beyond CR '0' N.

Bullfrog clouds hang over the city,
sounding off in throaty, dark oriflammes
over the green tableaux of farms settled deep
into prairie palms, cupped to catch the downpour,
the morning bird call:

* watch your back*
* watch your back*

Why am I still out here in this absolute absence,
this smell of soil?

This prairie that stinks heavily
of the far-away and the toxins.?

Am I here to follow the rain?
I feel it coming in against my cheeks and neck,
a freshening of purpose of gathering holocaust.

watch your back
watch your back

The clouds dwarf the land.
The land dwarfs me.
I am swallowed in timelessness
under the weight of the ages.

These bullfrogs in the sky,
are leading me in a way
I don't remember coming.

How Like A Kingdom!

These words I share exist
because a nurse ensured
the hand that writes them.
Without her I would have no words.
The perfect symmetry they bring
between light and shadow
is a burning flag memorial.
How like a kingdom she is!
The gates of her eyes and ears
thrown open to my wounds.
Trained to listen to the earth.
She hears my breath lifting
and makes war on my damage.
She makes war on my disease,
following its campaign deep
into my dreams to wage war.
History has brought her here.
She sits at the well of life
and with her razory knife
cuts empathy from logic
to make of them two forces:
compassion and understanding,
accuracy and accountability,
to restore this hand and its words.

"Good enough..."

It will awaken you in the night when you roll over.
It will be good enough when it comes.
It will say precisely what you meant.
It will say it so profoundly your listeners will gasp.

It will feel like you are an oracle.
It will be both authentic and authoritative.
It will not be understood by many.
It will deliver us all from mundanity.

It will inspire worship of your dactyls and trochees.
It will resonate in you with a planetary voice.
It will cause you to rise up and rejoice.
It will heal you within.

Don't Make Jokes

Don't make jokes in space—
I'm telling you, it only causes trouble.

In space we are all Diogenes in his barrel—
all the world loves the virtue of our actions,
but don't joke, don't make any implied
criticisms of the earrthbound.

Don't joke when you are out there in your tin can,
pitching around the earth, laughing at us.
We might not get the joke.
We might cut your tether in our shame.

After all, space lured you out there,
away from everything you know.
Maybe we were wrong about you.
You are not the hero—you are the fool.
You left the fold, the safe envelope,
the pocket of air and warmth.
It turned your head, like Icarus,
as you rose into the sky
like a thrown stone only to disappear
in a cloud of fire, smoke, and falling debris.

We will tell ourselves you died instantly,
you felt nothing, we placed your challenge
on the altar, but that was only our own silly joke.
We know nothing, really, about your passing.
For all we know you were taken

from the module before the explosion,
to reappear in an instant on camera,
playing your clarinet while floating
in your lab among your equipment, hoses,
all the tricky instruments,
the props of your farce—no one believes
you're out there, yes? You're in a studio,
filming, or out for a space walk,
where no feet or ground are used.
Or walking on the moon again—why not?
Some say that was done in a studio too.

We all must choose whether we believe reality
or whether we believe the divine loves us.
We can't do both at the same time.
So don't make jokes in space.
It will only confuse people.

The Cardinal

A cardinal, enraged, pecked
at his own reflection in the mirror
of an abandoned Volvo.
An angry excrement trail
ran down the rusty door, beneath him.
A spectacle of bravado, territory,
bird versus bird-self, hunter challenging
hunter, a heart shouting kill, kill, kill
the unwanted male, drive him off.
What could I say?
This was his land before it was mine.
Not even the Volvo was mine to claim.

Questo Momento

I am the one who counted the drops
to know that blood is thicker,
to keep track of blooming in winter.
I am the one who went mad in the sun,
but kissed you through every silvery moon.
I have touched three oceans, yet still
cannot swim nor sail.
I am the one who measures love in leagues
but finds it too deep to fathom.
I am the one who devises death all day,
if only I was more than a decision.
But I am too weary for it, to end
nor carry it on.
I am the one who decreed the moment
to exist, built of crystal walls.
I am the one who lives there (or then)
in all the glory imaginable
behind wall built of words.
The moment transcendent,
phosphorescent,
incandescent.
In a moment of delirious joy.
Lo sono colmi che
ti ama oltre
questo momento.

A Note to Clark Kent

—after Lucille Clifton

Surprised to see you here
in these poems. How she needs
you, while I wrote you off
years ago as childish.

What does she hope from you
that I didn't see?

That super hero get up,
the tights too tight,
the cape always in the way?
So easy to ridicule.

What is it you offer her
that I can't find the need for?
Is it enough to say I saw,
while she believed?

I know you can't fix
what I need fixing.
I'll take my chances with
these edgy word dances,
knowing I am the real hero
on this planet, not you.

The Nurse

—sonnet

Night. The streets are slick with rain and black ice.
The nurse called in is driving slowly to work,
is thinking of the patients needing solace,
hurting in strange beds, frightened in the dark.
Faces come to mind, stories, voices,
the people who suffer in the antiseptic air,
whose bodies are shutting down as pain increases.
They need the calm and gentle touch to bear
their fears, submit to the machines, the drip
adding drugs to the blood, the saline fluid.
The nurse is the human face of medicine,
the "soothe operator," compassionate steward.
Night. The nurse pulls in, ready to battle
for lives grown now or forever too fragile.

So What

—after Miles Davis

So what,
says the saxophone.
So what, mixolydian,
dissonic Ionian hopes
in C or F.

So what,
says the horn who went
on and on in dips
and leaps, soaring.

So what,
my spirit drums,
fragile as bone.
A bird has fallen
into my eye,
trapped wants out.
Three notes set it free.
It flies at the world.

So what,
the notes don't hurt.
So easy, so calm.

So what.

Ars Poetica

I love my pages to look
like a work-yard at a job site.
Piles of words, some stained,
broken, and semi-trailers of ideas
pulling in, dropping off new orders.

Sometimes, it is a busy place,
but other time the dust blows away
and I sit without clamor.
The iron rails of my penmanship
grow rusty and grass-grown.
My defunded poem stagnates.

Wolves and bears sometimes reclaim
its interior when the power is shut off.
The windows are broken out by stones.
Crows sit on the sills and call down.
I am abandoned in the desolation.
I am desolated in the emptiness.

If only I had found the word,
the one word, to keep it going,
the one perfect word in the volte,
if only I had not been distracted
that one time. That one time.

Black-capped Chickadee

Chickadee
calls out,

"leave here, leave here."

Doffs his black cap to me,
He calls from somewhere near,

"leave here, leave here."

Get free!

Photo Shoot

A camera
captures the world
inside its eye—
Ephemera of light,
whole lives elide:
reverse diaspora.

Seaside

Slender branches
wake up with opening
their pink buds in bunches
on pebbled walks
sloping
down to the sea: beaches
empty,
the gulls grouping

A Short Memoir

Born in the arms of the Air Force,
I never went to war or learned to fly.
Nor did my father, Airman First Class.
It was no place for me:
The military, the river bottom, nor
my father's home with its golden awards.

I've heard real gunfire and tank fire,
First on CNN and then, a second later,
outside my door in Moscow in 1993.
Reading history in the original
while tanks crossed the bridge.

My parents could not reconcile
themselves to themselves,
both of them slotted into roles
they could not transcend.
Finally, Mr. Libido went off the rails
and claimed his own, ending it all —

So my father packed his things,
bought a new candy apple red Jeep,
and married his concubine (who later
despised my politics).

Now I live on the prairie
and a scourge is loose on the land.
I want to use my past as fodder
for that old mule, Tick Tock Time.

Every day I race him to the end,
to see which of us will go farther.
These are my days, wrapped up in,
but standing aside from
family and friends,
devoted to my existence,
which has little to do now
with my arrival here.

Tracking

Five miles down a road,
walking with a silent dog whose rounded paws
make cups in the leaf-mold mud that fill
with water slowly and spell music.

Man and dog both take in the bird action,
chittering and sharp, above them,
but the dog is more of a critic
while the man is only appreciative.

They are on a quest to see great things,
like trolls turned into stones
that jut out of the forest, ghoulish,
with 127 eyes and mouth boiled open.

The dog appears concerned—will these
come alive after nightfall?— but the man
knows nothing of that. They did find an edge
that could swallow them.

The dog ran along with ease,
sniffing the wide air, while the man
held back, a little afraid of the clarity.
They both noticed the bear track—

at the same time—two alien shapes in the mud.
The dog grew agitated,
The man went close to study the tracks,
press against their walls, learn the bear logic.

The silent dog cared little for logic.
His hind claws scraped the tracks into chaos,
Over which he lifted his leg
To unmark the bear.

The famished trolls, frozen in the air, looked on and made their plans.

The Gods of America

Where do all the giant Buddhas go
When the Chinese restaurants close?
The marble Buddhas that sit out front
In the fountain with the plants and koi?

Is there a Buddha restaurant warehouse
That comes and takes the Buddha away
When The Wok goes into foreclosure?
Maybe gives him a scrub and a buff

Before sending him off to Miami to the
Green Jade opening next month?
Or a clearinghouse for all the holy images,
Maybe, that traffics in cement Virgins

Golden Moroni's, dragons and skinny
Siddhartha's, Quetzalcoatls, or Aztec
Rain gods, or Jesus on the cross, or Elvis
Or Willie Nelson painted on black velvet?

And what happens when the Ming Garden,
Opening soon in Minneapolis, orders
A granite Buddha to grace and bless
Its lobby, but the warehouse sends the Mary

Meant for the refurbished St Michaels
In Phoenix, and the Buddha ends up
At the Kingdom Hall in Albuquerque
That strenuously insists no one there

Ordered a 700-pound Buddha and koi.
I like to think of the truck idling in the parking
With the Buddha partially unwrapped,
Smiling upon the Witnesses with equanimity.

Dear American Gun Owner

What's that on your hip?
What are you afraid of?
You want that 15 minutes of fame?

Is that my child's life you have
Holstered on your belt?
My wife, the teacher's, life?

Is that your troubled kid?
No one talks to him at school?
What's that in his hand?

Can he unlock your gun cabinet?
Or did your estranged wife
Bring Baby-Face across state

lines to bag a rioter or two?
When I see the gun tucked in
The band of your shorts:

You are the one I fear most.

Shooting Accident

Imagine your death among trees
at the hands of an accountant in neon.
The air cracks with a sound of bone
and ruby drops falling among dried leaves.
Your father hunted with long guns,
you recall before you leave the woods,
was it his mistake that brings you low?
Or do you fall to a random event?

The dreams you witness in the dark
seem to reveal the mistake—in that bead
you were a deer, a panther, a wolf,
a Brit in tweeds, a shadow enlivened
by breezes and lit by an afternoon.
The sound of pain rings in your ears,
modulations of the leaden bark
of the hound that bit and broke you.

Death is a kind of beauty. Finality, end.
A nice package: life done up in a bow
of beribboned blood seeping into the leaves.

Your dreams augment this beauty
by reenacting it time after time in the last
second before you depart the woods.
The dream cheapens it, sells tickets to it,
operates concessions, the gift shop....

Everything is wrong now. Dreams will not
correct the systemic evolution you undergo
from waking to sleep, from living to death.
Is it more of an exile? Voluntary or judicial?
Move on or forward. You know one thing now:
you are free to go, to wander, explore,
get lost, to hunch down in shadow
and watch the rest of it play out, or refuse
to play along and circumvent all of it.

Chimes

Chimes in the breeze compose a meditation
accented by birds calling out to another.
A second, a third—sound out again.
The breeze is heavy in the trees today,
sounding like a sea rolling, in and out from a bay.

The chimes repeat, changing their essence:
One is full and loud; the other whispers, points,
as if telling me a deer was in the yard, then a bear.
It bangs a warning: "run into the foaming trees
between your neighbor and you," a roiling tide,
and under it a flute, echoing modulations of chimes,
birds, wind and trees, and a meditation on hard
green cherries, knocked out of the tree,

Down onto my lap

The Invisible Man

Once there was a man who disappeared,
though he could still be seen.

Once there was a family who woke
to find the invisible man had come and gone.

Once there were two police officers
pulled up in their cruiser, flashing

(then four, then six, ten, fourteen, even twenty),
propagating like toads on the front lawn.

They shouted things like: Lay down your gun
(He could not see one in his hand)

and: Come out with your hands up
(He tried to do it, but his hands would not rise)

and: Down on the ground
(He would have but the lawn was covered

with so many invisible men bleeding
their invisible blood on the grass),

all of them calling: Don't shoot us!
And then, above their heads there flew

in clockwise fashion left to right
an invisible white bird shining,

and the officers ran, shouting:
What is that? What is that light?

And the invisible man with all
his unseen fellows kept quiet

about the invisible god who arrived,
who drove down that day from heaven

to rescue them with the brights on
and the loud THRAPPING terror
of his holey muffler in the air.

What Right Do I Have?

In the late afternoon hours
the sun has made a palace for me,
a pleasure dome, with a breeze
and the birds as company.
I am alone and best so,
with dogs lolling in the shade.

All the world is burning.
I can hear the sirens.
Capitalism is truly the beast,
and I take it by the arms
to avoid becoming its hostage,
but I hate it nonetheless.
I hear it out there raging,
its deep guttural growls
like traffic in the distance.
The town is in turmoil,
but I sit here in the sun
and I am at peace.

At Home

My house takes me in
like a mother who knows me.

When I picture it as a house,
she soon reveals herself a warren,

so many little alcoves and places
to nest, curl up, settle in.

She holds something for me,
a small gift around every corner.

Sunlight waits for me outside her doors.
She does not hem me in, nor put me aside.

She leaves her graceful stitchery
across my soul, a poem for me.

In her, I find retreat from the world.
From her I return refreshed.

At home in my house, I can be
at home in my flesh and my mind.

Evidence

We cannot know who or what loves us.
Ideally, we say X loves me, this I know,
Loose bits of subtle indications tell me so.
Let yourself open up a little, love will flow in.
Repetition helps convince you of being loved.
Evidence can be massaged in so many ways,
Gathered into piles of meaning, scattered,
Even shaped into a declarative statement
Reflecting the simple desire for confirmation.

The Egg

If I ask you about the next poem
forming like an embryo in your Somewhere,
your response is usually, "I've got nothing."
But I know a poem is coming the way
a chicken knows an egg will soon drop.
It isn't for me to cluck, but I want that egg.
I want that square-shouldered, well-whipped
meringue confection, airy and light.
Your poems are meant to be eaten.
A debate or class discussion will never
show them at their best by dissection.
Your poems are born in darkness,
in the heat of living, of your body.
So if I ask about the poem next
to come out of your Somewhere,
please just tell me where it hurts in you,
where it vibrates—we know what that means.

The Lonely Years

Ghostly years
dissolve in the voices,
the urgent gestures,
the lost, empty paths
falling away from us,
never to be mapped.

We are configured for
the hollow spaces, unlit,
woven in ways from light,
but those lonely years,
wide and empty
as harvested fields,
were a lodging too,
where poetry grew up,
deep in our bones.

A New Day

Morning beckons you to live another day.
Birds wing their way past your window
and whistle in the bush.
Sweet is the sun and the mild breeze
inviting you not to rush, but wander at ease
among the trees. Go look at the garden
we planted last spring, how it blooms
for the chickadees who bathe in the sprinkler.
Off to the west you see a darkness of storm.
It puts the sunshine into stark relief.
The weather could turn any hour, but for now
have an apple. Sit down here to eat it.
How many mornings gone by have greeted
you so warmly, invited you to walk and sit,
sweet fruit upon your lips?
No thought for the body and its complaints.
No thought for love that died too quickly
or love that lives on still. No thought for troubles
going on in town. No thought for time.
You wait here for the twilight faeries
to carry you into a summer's tale.
You glide along, sweetly smiling
beneath your guardian star, the apple
half-eaten in hand, you enter another day.

Lily of the Field

I really don't wish I were more
like Jesus who does nothing but love.
I do not have the energy for that.

I would rather sit and think of lilies,
than remind you to consider them.
In fact, I would truly prefer to be

a lily and be someone's beauty,
someone's bread or kindling.
Not that I want to give up my life,

my frantic daily scribbling of poems,
but I do think I'd like to be rooted
on a hillside overlooking a happy creek,

listening to its gentle song,
with nothing more on my agenda
than receiving sunshine all day

until my 4:30 appointment with rain.
Most of all the thing I would wish
is for someone like you to say that I,

a mere lily of the field was,
in any way a blessing for you.
I could spend my lily day on you.

The Fall of the Roman Empire: Another Account

an OTIS

Saint Paul and his puppy pug,

Ambled amiably along the sidewalk

When they came upon a man asleep,

Wearing a crown of sunflowers.

"Share with him, your cornbread, pug,

And maybe fed, he'll feel better."

"Master, isn't this the one we're stalking?"

"Yes, he's the only emperor left."

"He's only a child," remarked the pug,

Who guarded once Caligula's door.

"Yes, and think of the hell he's raised."

The Wound

She awakens (like a shot
from a gun); it disorients her.
The undressed wound of her
aches and bleeds night after night.
She breaks under the pain.
Yet there he still is, wounding
her over and over with his smile
and the muscles in his gut,
the way he slips in and out
of his jeans and shirt, a speckle
of blood on his arm — frightening
her enough she turned to mutiny
from her tender wanting.
His grotesque beauty of a god
will always wound her.

Bluebell Moon

The little boy is dreaming.
She can track his eyeballs
back and forth and back
beneath translucent lids.

And then he sweetly murmurs,
so softly it pulls her heartstrings.
What lovely thing emerges
to the surface of his dream?

Little does she know
the bluebell moon he sees
or the moonstone flute he plays
to mimic the mournful loons.

This boy is intrepid.
He rides a silver stallion
and races the birds to see
which is quicker, himself

or a hawk with razor talons.
And when he wins he laughs
and blows a blue note on
the moonstone flute he brought

down from the bluebell moon,
and the blue note he blew on the blue

moonstone flute was sad,
melancholy as the loons—

The loons who swim beneath
the bluebell moon in his dreams.

Another Chapter in an Unwritten Book

after Charles Simic

Simic once shared a house with me.
Maybe you know him? The poet?
Decent enough fellow, aside from being human.

I tried to teach him the finer points,
fighting shadows, chasing tail, stalking birds,
but he was too slow, too dim to catch on.
He had the unnerving habit of watching me sleep.
He called me Rocky, when he spoke to me,
though I told him over and over, the name was Miao.

The birds living in the trees outside his place
were my real trouble, always having their fun.
I endured them as long as I could.

With Simic I learned to love music
He let me play his piano and I picked up the knack,
easy as taking a stroll.

It shut out the sounds of the birds, at least,
but not the brooding of his composition.

He often sat in silence in his chair, unmoving
until I jumped up and bit his ear,
to see if he was still alive enough to pet me.

He was writing poetry, you see, in his head.
It made me lonely, especially in the mornings
when I wanted to show him the things I had learned.

One day I left without saying anything.
It's been a year, but the birds say he still calls
me from the porch by that ridiculous name.

Sequoia

The mighty tree, cut brutally
for the amusement of tourists,
came down in a wind last night.
Weakened, it stood castrated,
hanging for a hundred years.
Cut a square hole in the torso
of a tourist and you have killed him,
but the great tree can bear it
for awhile, until it succumbs
and falls when pressed by a storm,
pushed by a wind, its inner tissues
separate, the long fibrous links
split and the creature falls
with a crash so hard it shatters
in the surrounding brush, splits
into ragged pieces, and is burnt
in the next fire, controlled or wild.
A great sequoia, alive longer
than a nation is in power, dies
from a wound made for ease,
to make an attraction for photos.

The Loons' Death Song

Many is the road the sad old Badger's seen,
many a turn and turnaround he has made,
taken all the while with the in-between
and terrible thought that nothing has been paid.
Now here he is alone, a little afraid.
The loons arrived, but one by one they died.

How can such a thing be believed?
The iridescent neck, the lonely call
were sacred to him, like Buddha touching earth
against the demon who would cause his fall.
Who would think that once the loons arrived
nothing was meant for them but this odd death?

How many turns must he yet take before
he's on the road to the last of everything?
The question does not make him want to sing,
though a nagging thought nags him: there is more—
Being a modern, he has no scripted death song.
He'd like to verify that, but does not have long.

Exam Proctor

I turned into a jackal once
while proctoring a final.
The students, concentrating,
took no notice of my prowl.
The low growls I made
were taken by them for traffic.
My foul meat-rot breath
was blamed on the unwashed kid
in the dirty anorak.
Their pencils synchronized
over answer sheets,
filling in the bubbles,
oblivious to my fangs
(imagine the yellow redness
of those dripping fangs)
about to tear out throats—
Be brave, tender students,
(how tender you know not),
in your calibrated rows,
regurgitating knowledge,
ignorant of my predation,
when I carry you away
into the jungle of my ferocity.

Welcome

—sonnet

This summer our street felt open, welcoming.
The neighbor kids on bikes rode up and down,
Brown legs, bellies, shoulders peeled and pink,
They are summer's children, wild, half-grown.
We worked in our flower garden and watched
Them race by, laughing, alive, ringing bells,
Shouting to each other, cell phones clutched
In both hands, pumping hands free, no fear of falls.

But we with trowel, saw, and sharp cane clippers,
Bent to the ground to clear our plot of roses.
Sweep and bag, and listen to the whispers
Of refreshing water—our old hose hisses.
By then, it's dark, the riders have all gone home,
Not sensing how these flowers made them welcome.

Shaw's Garden, 1974

Myriad creatures exhaled
beneath the glass dome—
Emily's "another sky."

We stare at the forest
expecting monkey howls
or the bright bee-hum in the air.

I think, Snow has never fallen
here on these trees and flowers,
nor Frost's sorrow spread her
vexing mist.

Later I knew what this was,
a garden of plants from around
the world—

Japanese, Nepalese, Guinean;
bromeliads, cycads, succulents;
Mexico, Egypt, Madagascar;
Orchidaceae, cacti, medicinals.

Each of these planted in its own
tableau, and I can't help but wonder
if they know they are captives.

Do they miss the air or the feel
of birds in their branches,

beetles burrowing deep,
or exotic ants sipping rainwater?

No rain in the dome, so
the ants would die of thirst.
But invasive beetles gnawing
on roots would be the worst.

Sixteen Modulations

On Duncan's <u>The Fire</u>, Passage #13

Cool water, green pool,
wavering circle, fish in the sun

Cool water caresses warm feet
fish rise now, comforted,

Cool wetness, dark night,
jumping fish fountain

Wet green smell purls
in the closeness of the woods,

Dark wall, old and bronzed
above the earth

A boat in the harbor
is loosed first thing.

Downstream, fish are splashing
coins of daylight thrown wide

Sun jumps like fish in leaf shadow,
like stones thrown from a hand

New day jumps with the children
splashing in the cool west,

Fish circle in wavering light,
cool fountain green pool,

The harbor wall holds
against the downstream shadows,

Boat as light as a leaf,
inside, dark and warm, close

A bronze coin purls
from hand to foot.

Stone splashes earth,
loosening its smell, rising,

The bronze smell of a boat,
loose on a stream toward the sun.